# kenosis
## living like Jesus in an upside-down world
a devotional journal through the book of Philippians

Derek Neider & Fernando Serrano

**Special Thanks**

We want to give special thanks to all those who helped make this journal a reality:

Crissy Hatherly, Tristan Agasi,
Natalie Serrano, Lorena Molina

@2024 Awaken Las Vegas
**awakenlv.org**
You are welcome to visit in person at
7175 W. Oquendo Road Las Vegas, Nevada 89113

Dear Reader:

You are invited to use this devotional journal as you listen to the sermons from this series at any time, either in person or online.

All proceeds from the sale of this book are dedicated to Awaken Events. These are large-scale evangelistic outreaches around the world for the purpose of spreading the gospel and awakening souls to the light of Christ. Please visit awakenevents.org to learn more.

Scan for sermons and
interactive elements

# Introduction

It has been said that spiritual awakenings result from God's grace during social and cultural upheaval. If you study spiritual awakenings, you know this to be the case both in the Biblical testimony and church history. It is fair to ask what it is about social calamity that often initiates a dynamic work of God. Think about what you know in Scripture as a starting point. It was when Israel was burdened under the weight of Pharaoh's ungodly government and his persecutions that God sent His Redeemer. This kicked off a world-renowned exodus filled with dynamic supernatural events that have forever identified the children of Israel as God's people. It all began with one simple, collective cry from the Israelites, recorded in Exodus 2:23-25, "During those many days the king of Egypt died, and the people of Israel groaned because of their slavery and cried out for help. Their cry for rescue from slavery came up to God. And God heard their groaning, and God remembered his covenant with Abraham, with Isaac, and with Jacob. God saw the people of Israel—and God knew." Moreover, this pattern of social calamity leading to a collective pursuit of God is found throughout the Book of Judges and follows this pattern: God's people walk with Him faithfully, experience His rich blessings, become comfortable, turn away from God, turn to false idols, their society falls apart, they cry out to God, God brings a spiritual awakening. In a more modern context, this has been the pattern in the United States. Every Great Awakening has been preceded by a time of waywardness among God's people and subsequent social conflict. When people cry out to God, He answers them in phenomenal ways. This is the origin story of our tribe, Calvary Chapel.

We chose Philippians as our study because it is our conviction that we are living in one of those moments that has the radical potential to erupt into another spiritual awakening. Awakenings begin among God's children when their hearts return to their Redeemer. That is precisely what this book is about. It is not about five steps to a joyful life or finding joy during difficulty. While those themes are contained within, Philippians is much deeper than that one-dimensional approach. This book teaches us how to live right-side-up in an upside-down world. It teaches us that Jesus, the incomparable Son of God, who radiates divinity, was willing to empty Himself and condescend, for humanity's sake and the glory of the Father, by becoming a man, a servant, and experiencing physical death, even the death of the cross. Through His humble condescension, He made atonement and has become the Redeemer of humanity and all creation. Furthermore, as Christ's followers, His work in our lives is transformational as we now follow in His footsteps, living out His humble example in every aspect of our lives. This is an example in radical conflict with the world that we live in.

It is our prayer that God's Spirit will work in our hearts individually and as the Awaken community, transforming us increasingly into the image of Jesus. Furthermore, by our determination to follow Christ's example, the world will see that Jesus is uniquely able to satisfy our hearts, lead us to a flourishing life, and enable us to live out humanity as God intended. Moreover, this would draw them to Christ, and we would see the spiritual awakening, we have prayed for, come to Las Vegas, our nation, and the world through the love of Jesus, one person at a time.

Derek Neider and Fernando Serrano

# The Epistle to the Philippians

## Fascinating Features

While Philippians isn't as long or theologically intricate as some of Paul's other epistles, it has many extraordinary features. It was penned with three other epistles while Paul was imprisoned in Rome and is considered the most personal of the Pauline epistles. It was written to the first church that Paul founded in Europe, which was initially composed of an Asian from Thyatira, a Greek soothsayer whom God saved from demonism, and a Roman jailer whom God saved from emperorism. Furthermore, it contains what is considered by some to be the earliest Christian hymn (2:5-11).

For centuries, this epistle has encouraged God's people during hardship to be content in every circumstance, to use their minds in ways that lead to life, not death, and to find joy in Jesus.

## The Planting of the Church

Paul's relationship with the church at Philippi was extraordinary, starting with the unique guidance of God upon the missionary team, who led them to this unique Roman city. According to Acts 16, Paul and Silas had been visiting the churches in Asia Minor that Paul and Barnabas previously planted. Picking up young Timothy in Lystra, they had determined to continue their ministry in Phrygia and Galatia but were somehow forbidden by the Holy Spirit. As they continued their journey, coming to Mysia, they intended to further their efforts in Bithynia but were again not permitted by the Spirit of Jesus. That very night, a Macedonian man appeared to Paul in a vision, urging the team to come to Macedonia to help them. Recognizing this as the leading of God, they set sail, traveling eventually to the city of Philippi. The geographic significance of this decision cannot be overstated as the gospel was, perhaps for the first time, finding its way into Europe and gradually the Western world.

Paul's typical method of evangelizing a new city was to begin in the Jewish synagogue. However, apparently because of the absence of a quorum of 10 Jewish men, there was no synagogue in Philippi, so on the Sabbath, the missions team made their way to a place of prayer by a river where they encountered women praying and shared the gospel with them. Among them was a wealthy woman named Lydia, a businesswoman from Thyatira who sold purple goods. God opened her heart, she received Jesus, was baptized, and received the missions team as guests in her home. Continuing their ministry, Paul exorcised a demon from a slave girl and, with Silas, was dragged into the marketplace, and was accused of resisting the customs and religion of the Romans. After being severely beaten with rods and thrown into the innermost prison, the prison was miraculously shaken by an earthquake as they prayed and sang hymns, leading to the Philippian jailer surrendering his life to Jesus. This band of new believers: Lydia, her family, the Philippian jailer, his family, and presumably the young slave girl, composed the church's core in Philippi.

## Paul's Relationship to the Church

From the beginning, Paul's relationship with the church was one of friendship. Commentators and scholars view Paul's epistle to Philippi as a friendship letter. These Philippian Christians held a special place in the Apostle's heart, evidenced in the initial words that he shared with them. Far from purely sentimental, Paul reflected on the inception of this church with warm affection and regularly brought them before the Father in prayer. For their part, the believers in Philippi also held the Apostle close to their hearts. They respected him as a spiritual leader, believed in his apostolic calling, and faithfully supported his ministry efforts financially, even while he lingered under house arrest in Rome, which became the occasion for the penning of this epistle.

## The Occasion of Paul's Writing

Paul didn't write this epistle from the beauty of the beaches along the Mediterranean or the comforts of a chalet in the mountains of Cappadocia. Paul was under house arrest in Rome, having made his appeal to Caesar. His journey to this point was marked by a riot in Jerusalem, murderous attempts by the Sanhedrin, two years of prison in Caesarea, violent storms at sea, a shipwreck on the island of Malta, and being bitten by a snake. Now, in Rome, a much longed-for destination by the untiring, Paul awaited his audience with Caesar. Of course, Paul's time was not spent in idle waste. Paul industriously advanced the gospel, leading the Imperial Guard and many in Caesar's household to faith (1:13; 4:22). While daily chained to a rotation of Roman soldiers, Paul penned this epistle along with epistles to the churches in Ephesus, Colossi, and a letter to his friend Philemon. Paul took this opportunity to thank the believers in Philippi for their generous financial gift that came at the hands of Epaphroditus. He also addressed a relational disruption between two women leaders in the church, Euodia and Syntyche (4:2-3).

## Central Theme

The book's theological center is what many have called the "Christ Hymn" (2:5-11) and is believed to be an early-church song that was often sung in the community of God's people. This section of Scripture, rich in Christology expresses the self-giving love of God through the progressive condescension of Christ. It begins with equality with God, moves downward through the incarnation and the lowly position of a bondservant, and reaches its culmination in the deepest depths of death, specifically crucifixion—the ultimate expression of shame and contempt in the Roman world. This profound hymn's epicenter is the Son's humble willingness to empty Himself. The Greek word used for empty is kenosis. By using this word, Paul means that Jesus chose not to exploit His divine power for His own purposes in retribution, exaltation, or self-protection, as the emperors of Rome were accustomed to. Rather, He chose humility, a divine attribute which esteemed the needs of others and that of salvation, over His divine right to fight the world's power with a demonstration of divine power. He manifested a mightier power than that of raw strength. A power that came through humble love. In other words, He did what came naturally for God to do; He humbly gave Himself to make atonement for humanity and creation. Therefore, the emptying was not a divestiture of self-limitation but a robust metaphor for total self-abandonment and self-giving for the sake of others. This is what we will refer to as the cruciform life. The word cruciform means cross-shaped. It is the calling of every Jesus follower to form their life like Jesus, denying themselves, picking up their cross, and following Him (Matthew 16:24).

This example is precisely what Paul points to for Christians to form themselves after in relationship to one another. He prefaces the "Christ Hymn" with the appeal for Christians to have the same mind that was theirs in Christ (2:4-5), proceeding to exemplify the greatest example of choosing the attribute of humility and esteeming others even above self as an expression of true power demonstrated through what the world would perceive as weakness. This heavenly framework is thoroughly upside down from the world's point of view. Christ's humility unleashed the power of His love at the cross, which was the ultimate symbol of Rome's power over people. Christ's cross became the instrument through which principalities and powers, while seeking to silence and destroy the Holy One of Israel, became their undoing. At the same time, His cross was established as the instrument through which humanity and the world would be redeemed from the requirements of the law. Paul would connect these points when he said in Colossians 2:13-15, "And you, who were dead in your trespasses and the uncircumcision of your flesh, God made alive together with him, having forgiven us all our trespasses, by canceling the record of debt that stood against us with its legal demands. This he set aside, nailing it to the cross. He disarmed the rulers and authorities and put them to open shame by triumphing over them in him."

This power through weakness motif is eternally evident as the heavenly host will forever worship the Father and the Lamb. Notice that in His celestial Kingdom, the Lamb will rule and reign (Revelation 22:1-5). Jesus Christ, seen as the Lamb in Heaven, forever fuses humility and abnegation with flourishing and exaltation. It is precisely because of this extraordinary demonstration of humble love that the Father subsequently exalts His Son to the highest height, higher than any potentate, principality, or power. This gives Him the name above every name, which every created being will be required to humbly bow before and confess. Paul presents this not only as a Christological reality that compels us to worship Him but as a present-day model for us to live towards and follow. It is the kenosis of Christ that solves the puzzles of life from Heaven's perspective. Every aspect of Paul's writing in this book is tied to this theme.

## Outline of the Book

The arrangement and outline of this book are unique compared to Paul's other epistles. The seven sections are centralized around the theme of kenosis, God's true power exemplified through Jesus' exercise of humble love (2:5-11). Every point the Apostle makes is directly tied back to this model that Jesus lived. Joy, a flourishing life, healthy relationships, purpose in adversity, having a healthy view of our lives, correct thinking, and contentment are ours to experience when we abandon the temptation to use power for our selfish purposes and instead humble ourselves for the sake of others. This is how a Christian lives right-side-up in an upside-down world.

Simply put, we are naturally inclined and socially formed to think of ourselves first, position ourselves above others, and use our resources to gain the greatest advantage for our interests. Christ's life teaches us to do the exact opposite. Living this life, the cruciformed life, empowers the Christian community to be God's city set on a hill, a light shining in the great darkness, beckoning people to come to Jesus. It is through the cruciformed life that we indeed are

Christians, a term the unbelievers in Syrian Antioch used to describe believers as little Christs.

In light of this, the sections of this epistle are like spokes on a wheel, connected back to the key section (2:5-11). The sections are as follows:

Section 1
Love Others in Adversity (1:11)

Section 2
Discover Joy and Purpose in an Upside-Down World (1:12-26)

**Section 3**
**Jesus, the Cruciformed Life and Real Power (1:27-2:18)**

Section 4
Follow People Who Follow Jesus (2:19-30)

Section 5
Seeing Your Life Through the Gospel of Christ (3:21)

Section 6
Right Side Up Your Thinking (4:1-9)

Section 7
Living a Content Life in Christ (4:10-23)

## Context of the City of Philippi

As a Roman colony, Philippi held significant status in Macedonia. Named after the father of Alexander the Great, Philip of Macedon, the city boasted a rich history. Eventually, it became a destination for discharged soldiers who had served in the Roman army and were ready for retirement. Like most Roman colonies, a plurality of religions was accommodated, with the religious focus centralized around emperor worship. Along with the zeal to worship the Roman emperor, came also a commitment to the Roman way of life, or the Pax Romana (Roman peace). Paul equipped these Christians directly to deal with these two challenging aspects of their context by reinforcing the Lordship of Jesus Christ (2:10-11) and the peace of God that comes through Jesus (4:6-7).

## Go Deeper Resources

Available Sunday Teachings: This journal is intended to complement the Sunday morning messages taught at Awaken. If you miss the study, you can scan this code or visit *awakenlv.org/kenosis*.

# Blue Letter Bible

When studying Scripture, there are tools that will aid in unlocking Bible truths. First, reading the section of Scripture in various translations can be helpful. Second, utilizing reference tools to do word studies and connect you to other similar or relevant Scriptures will deepen your knowledge of God's Word. An excellent online tool called Blue Letter Bible provides these resources and more at no cost. Visit *blueletterbible.org*.

# Lectio Divina

The single most effective tool for revealing the richness of this epistle is an ancient approach to reading Scripture called Lectio Divina. Pastor Derek uses this method in the Daily Devotional, which you can find a link to using the QR code or visit *awakenlv.org/kenosis*. Follow these steps to study the verses in each journal entry.

- Prepare your heart before God by directing your attention to Him in a time of silence and prayer.

- Ask God to reveal Himself and give you spiritual understanding as you read.

- Meditate on Scripture by slowly and thoughtfully reading the verses, paying close attention to what God's Spirit highlights in your mind and heart.

- Pray again that your understanding will go deeper.

- Slowly and thoughtfully reread the verses.

- Journal what God has revealed to you, making specific and concrete applications to your life and actions you can take.

# How to Use This Journal Effectively

We have included step-by-step guidance for each journal entry to maximize your study of Philippians. The following explains how to utilize each step most effectively.

## Pray

Prayer plays an essential role in your pursuit of God. Praying before and during your Bible study prepares your heart to receive all God has for you by getting you on "the same page" as His Spirit. It sets the tone by helping you to set your mind on things above and by bringing your will into subjection to the God who loves you and is shaping you into the image of His Son. As C.H. Spurgeon said, "Prayer prepares your heart to be saturated with the dew of Heaven."

## Meditate

This describes a more profound, focused time of thinking and reflecting on a specific verse or verses from the teaching. Unlike worldly meditation methods, Biblical meditation is not an act of emptying your mind of thoughts. It is the opposite; it is filling your mind and heart with God's Word, giving the Spirit space to speak to you. We suggest you read the focus verses several times and commit them to memory.

## Go Deeper

Go deeper in your study of the section of Scripture. Look closer to find connected verses that will expand your understanding of the theme and deepen your grasp of the Bible. Use the questions provided to provoke your thinking beyond a cursory reading, making an effort to consider the whole context of God's Word.

## Live It

In his epistle, James strongly encourages people to hear the Word and do it. Ask God to help you live His Word out. In other words, you should put into action what God has shown you. Application is one of the most critical aspects of reading and studying God's Word. If we do not apply its message, we can become little more than depositories for Bible data. As D.L. Moody said, "The Bible was not given for your information but for your transformation."

# section 1:
## Love Others in Adversity (1:1-11)

Paul was no stranger to adversity. In fact, he seemed to have a remarkable ability to avoid self-centered tendencies, victimization, and self-pity when circumstances were the hardest. Instead, he thought of others in his pain, prayed for them, and directed them to Jesus. It is natural to imagine Paul using his time to complain about his imprisonment, but instead, he actively wrote instructive letters to the people and churches he cared for. Of course, Paul modeled this upside-down way of responding to adversity after the true pioneer of selfless, others-centered living; Jesus Christ. Paul could champion Christ's cause in the lives of others because He experienced Christ championing it in his own.

### study 1
Philippians 1:1-2
Think of Others

### study 2
Philippians 1:3-6
Christ Your Champion

### study 3
Philippians 1:7-11
Aim to Abound in Love

# study 1

## Philippians 1:1-2
## Think of Others

The call to follow Christ involves self-denial, yet our natural inclination is self-centeredness. Each morning, we wake consumed with meeting our needs, satisfying desires, and pursuing dreams. This focus intensifies during challenging times like illness, loss, or economic hardship.

Reflecting on a friend's letters from prison, which often resembled shopping lists for items from toothpaste to books, I empathized deeply with his situation. In similar circumstances, I might have made similar requests. In contrast, Paul's letter to the Philippians, scribed from his imprisonment, demonstrates a different ethos. Instead of self-focus, Paul's words convey love, intentional prayer, and a spirit of self-denial. He exemplified Christ's love by prioritizing the needs of others above his own.

The world needs to see love in action; the only ones capable of exemplifying it are the followers of Christ. We have received the love of God and the power of the Spirit to prioritize others, identifying ourselves as citizens of Heaven.

## Pray

Spend dedicated time in prayer, seeking divine guidance for creative ways to prioritize others above yourself. Express gratitude for Jesus' sacrificial love and intercede for a specific need within the body of Christ.

## Meditate

Selfishness prioritizes personal gain; selflessness prioritizes the well-being of others without seeking personal benefit in return. As you consider this contrast, meditate on how Christ's selflessness impacts your life and future.

## Go Deeper

Scriptures: 1 Corinthians 10:24; 1 Peter 3:8; 1 Thessalonians 5:15; Galatians 5:14

If you were to put into practice loving your neighbor as yourself, what would be some of the new initiatives you would undertake toward others?

How do selflessness and humility enhance a Christian's usefulness for the kingdom?

## Live It

Start at home. This week, demonstrate your concern for others by assisting or alleviating the burden of a family member. Then, extend this initiative to your workplace and church community.

# study 2
## Philippians 1:3-6
## Christ Your Champion

To be sure, confidence is a critical component that leads to a flourishing life. Basketball players are taught to have confidence in their shot, salespeople in their charisma, and CEOs in their capacity to steer large organizations. "Psychology Today,"[1] Sounds pretty important, doesn't it? But is that what the Bible means when it speaks of confidence, and is our confidence meant to be centered on ourselves?

Confidence is the belief that one can rely on someone or something: a firm trust. The Bible, unsurprisingly, has a different view of where our confidence should be placed and where true happiness and a flourishing life come from. According to these verses in Philippians, our confidence should not be placed in ourselves; it should be placed in Jesus Christ. Paul emphasized that Christians can be sure, convinced, and even persuaded that the One who began the good work is also the One who will complete it. The incarnation, life, suffering, and resurrection of Jesus thoroughly convince us to rest our confidence in Christ for every aspect of our lives. While the world looks inward for stability and strength, the Christian looks to Jesus, the unchanging and Almighty One who alone is worthy of our absolute confidence. This is yet another way Christians live right-side-up in an upside-down world.

## Pray

Ask God to show you any way that you may have misplaced your confidence in something other than Him. Spend time confessing your trust in Jesus and dependence upon Him for everything. As you pray, make a list of those things you are entrusting to Him and allow your trust in God to build within you a Christ-confidence.

## Meditate

Focus on Philippians 1:6. Consider what the Bible means when it says that Jesus began a good work in you and what it means when it says He will complete it. What does this mean concerning your security as a believer?

## Go Deeper

Scriptures: Hebrews 12:1-2; Psalm 138:8; 1 Thessalonians 5:24; Romans 8:31-39

What responsibilities do you have as a Jesus follower who lives with Christ-confidence? For example, does this mean you passively expect God to work in your life? How do you actively engage in discovering and living God's will?

How does resting your confidence in Christ protect you from fear?

## Live It

Journal at least three ways you will develop a stronger confidence in Jesus. Be specific about the concrete steps you will take. This may include resisting current temptations to trust in people or worldly resources.

# study 3
## Philippians 1:7-11
## Aim to Abound in Love

The Christ-centered life makes you a person of love. Paul's prayer for followers of Christ is that they will have a love that abounds. The Greek word for "abound" implies something exceeding expectations and surpassing norms. Without a doubt, Paul tells us that God's children must exhibit a love that breaks with the world's and society's schemes. This love is found only in an intimate relationship with Jesus Christ. It is expressed in wisdom and knowledge, impacting decision-making and morality, resulting in a life that honors God.

## Pray

As you pray, express gratitude for God's extravagant love towards you. Ask God to reveal areas where you can deepen your love for Him and others. Allow yourself to be enveloped in His presence.

## Meditate

Loving God and others amidst adversity poses one of our greatest challenges. Reflect on verses 8-9, observing how Paul intertwines emotions, prayer, intellect, and discernment to depict the love we require.

## Go Deeper

Scriptures: 1 Corinthians 14:1; 1 Timothy 6:11; 2 Timothy 2:22

If you were to practice loving your neighbor as yourself, what would be some of the ways in which the biblical call to pursue love differs from society's perspective on love-seeking?

Why do Christians emphasize that God's love pursues us, and how does this inspire those seeking love?

## Live It

This week, creatively express your love for God or gratitude for His love.

Write a poem or song, create a painting, or capture an image on your phone. Share your expression of love by visiting *awakenlv.org/kenosis*

# key points from section 1

# section 2:

## Discover Joy and Purpose in an Upside-Down World (1:12-26)

The storms of life tend to throw us off course, dampening our spirits with clouds of adversity. We can feel abandoned by God and hopelessly lost as we are tossed about and turned upside down in our trials. The Christian life offers an antidote to these feelings. In Paul's life, we see that even while the storm was raging, there were the ever-present realities of purpose and joy rooted in the life of Christ and His promises. Joy and purpose are yours to discover and experience through the One who is the true reason for living and for the purpose of advancing His gospel.

### study 4

Philippians 1:12-18
Gospel Purpose

### study 5

Philippians 1:19-26
The Meaning of Life

# study 4
## Philippians 1:12-18
## Gospel Purpose

When hardship hits you, how do you handle it? The pain of trials and tribulations can seem arbitrary, tempting us to wonder how things that hurt so severely can serve a purpose. There's probably more than once when you have wondered how God could be working in your adversity. Society and culture often reinforce these feelings, encouraging us to insulate ourselves and avoid hardships, viewing them as counterproductive. However, these verses reveal that Paul had discovered a significant secret and advantage for Jesus' followers. As we center our lives around the kenosis of Christ, His willingness to empty Himself to fulfill the mission of God, and as we follow His example in this, we discover that even adversity can be used to serve God's purposes. We conclude, there is a purpose for everything in our lives, even the hard stuff. God can use the hard stuff, like Paul's imprisonment, to not only uniquely advance the gospel but to instill Christ-confidence in others as they observe God's faithfulness in our adversities, which encourages them to live boldly as gospel proclaimers in their challenging circumstances. Not only was gospel influence spreading into Caesar's household, but Paul's friends and enemies were spurred to a greater boldness to speak the Word.

Paul's momentary affliction was working a greater glory. It is truly a template for God's work in the lives of His servants.

## Pray

Ask God to strengthen you during times of trial to trust that He is working purpose in your adversity, that you will recognize the good things that He is doing, and that you will be bold to press on in faithfulness with what He has called you to. Pray that God will enable you to resist the temptation of the devil to quit or turn away from God's will.

## Meditate

Focus your attention on Philippians 1:12-14. Consider what it must have taken for Paul to press on in faithfulness as he was under house arrest for two years. Consider the other aspects of Paul's suffering throughout his life and how he responded.

## Go Deeper

Scriptures: Genesis 50:20; Job 42:5-6; Jonah 2:1-10; 1 Peter 5:10

What examples are there in the Bible of God's servants being taken through suffering to fulfill God's plan?

How did they respond? What were the keys to their success? How does this encourage you?

## Live It

Everyone is either going through trials or being prepared for one. Write down your strategy for dealing with trials so that you can be successful in spreading the gospel.

# study 5
## Philippians 1:19-26
## The Meaning of Life

For Paul, life, death, and eternity intersected at every moment of his walk with Christ. The secret to Paul's abundant life was having Christ as his center, strength, and motivation in each experience. For followers of Christ, life's purpose is serving Him, death is transitioning to Him, and eternity is enjoying Him. Embracing this reality enables us to structure our present like Paul did, choosing excellence over the good, difficulty over ease, and spiritual progress over personal complacency.

## Pray

In prayer, ask God to reveal the true meaning of life according to His design.

## Meditate

Compare Philippians 1:21 with the words of a missionary to India, Henry Martyn: "If God has work for me to do, I cannot die." Meditate on the work that God has for you in your family, work area, community, and church.

## Go Deeper

Scriptures: Ecclesiastes 12:13-14; 2 Timothy 4:1-5; Matthew 6:33

Based on the preceding verses, what truth have you discovered concerning the meaning of life.

In contemporary society, the most prevalent definition of the meaning of life often revolves around the pursuit of happiness, fulfillment, and personal success, as well as the accumulation of wealth and experiences. How does the biblical definition of the meaning of life surpass that of society?

## Live It

This week, explore a new facet of life's meaning by volunteering at church, LV Reach, or another community service organization. (*lvreach.org*)

# section 3:
## Jesus, the Cruciformed Life and Real Power (1:27-2:18)

New ageism suggests that emotional and spiritual wellness results from centering yourself through breathing exercises, positive thinking, and healing rituals. However, Christianity has an altogether different center; His name is Jesus. The core of this small but powerful epistle is found in Chapter 2, verses 5-11. In fact, these verses were sung as a hymn in the early church. A song recalling the profound downward condescension of Christ and His unparalleled ascension and exaltation. They are truly some of the most profound Christological verses in the Bible.

Paul's letter encourages believers in Philippi to count one another as more significant and to esteem the interests of others as higher—not as a recipe the world advocates for a fulfilled life. This seemingly incredulous request is exemplified in Jesus' incarnation and condescension and is the secret to a flourishing life. To put it in simpler terms, according to the Bible, the way up is down.

### study 6
Philippians 1:27-30
Politics in the Church

### study 7
Philippians 2:1-4
Be Like Jesus

### study 8
Philippians 2:5-8
The Crucified God

### study 9
Philippians 2:9-11
The Resurrected and Exalted Lord

### study 10
Philippians 2:12-18
Shut Up and Shine

# study 6
## Philippians 1:27-30
## Politics in the Church

In some circles, saying that politics matters in the church would be construed as a highly controversial statement. But the truth is Paul believed politics mattered. Let me explain. In Philippians 1:27, Paul tells this church that their manner of life, or their politic of life, mattered immensely. The word manner is based on a Greek word from which we derive our English word politics. Politics refers to structures designed to manage, regulate, or run society. So, what is Paul saying? He is saying that how you manage and run your life matters. And not only that, but the standard that you aim for as a Christ follower couldn't be higher. According to Paul, that standard is the value or worth of the gospel. In other words, your life should reflect the beauty, love, and power of God's story in all He did to redeem humanity and creation from the curse through Jesus, His Son. Not only is that the goal and aim of every Christian, but it is also the unifying goal of the Christian community. Above all things, the gospel's advancement unites us, motivates us, and serves our ultimate purpose. Now, this doesn't mean that other areas of activism in the church aren't necessary. Still, nothing is superior to or replaces living out God's mission of reaching the world with the gospel of Jesus and making disciples of all nations.

Does how you live your life and make choices demonstrate the worth of Christ's gospel in all He did for you?

## Pray

Pray that God will unite and strengthen your church as you prioritize the Great Commission. Pray for a fresh season of unity in heart and mission.

## Meditate

Focus on Philippians 1:29. Meditate on what Paul means when he tells the Christians at Philippi that they had been granted to suffer for His sake. Is suffering something the New Testament believers expected?

## Go Deeper

Scriptures: Matthew 28:18-20; Matthew 16:17-19; Mark 16:15-18

What gets in the way of churches prioritizing the advancement of the gospel? How do churches become distracted?

During Christ's earthly ministry, how did He emphasize the church's mission to reach the world with the gospel?

## Live It

Prioritize living the gospel in your life for the sake of the lost but also for the encouragement of the church. Be a uniting force for God's mission in the church and encourage other Christians to live out the Great Commission. Talk to a church leader about LV Reach or one of our upcoming mission trips. Take a step of faith.

# study 7
## Philippians 2:1-4
## Be Like Jesus

October 6th is "World Communion Sunday," a day dedicated to honoring Jesus Christ as the Head of the Church. It serves as a reminder that every Christian denomination promoting Jesus is part of one unified body. While the concept of uniformity may seem attractive, attempts to enforce it, as seen in historical dictatorships like the Russian regime or the Nazi movement, inevitably lead to chaos. However, unity of mind, love, agreement, humility, and valuing others highly reflect the essence of Christ and the unity of the Godhead. The uniqueness of Christ's community lies in His character. In the local church, genuine affection, fellowship, and worship become meaningful when participants embody Jesus' heart and character. Paul encourages us to emulate the mind of Jesus, enabling us to live as citizens of Heaven on earth and introduce others to God's kingdom of unity and love.

## Pray

Enter into a moment of meditative prayer. Contemplating Jesus' character, ask God to instill in you the desire to emulate Him and to treat others as He would. Additionally, pray for God's blessings upon any local Christian church you know.

## Meditate

Reflect on Jesus's profound impact during His time on earth, reread the text, and meditate on the potential impact you could have by becoming an imitator of Christ and treating others as He would.

## Go Deeper

Scriptures: Ephesians 5:1-2; 1 John 2:6; 1 Peter 4:1-2

How do the principles of unity, humility, love, and sacrificial living outlined in the previous references intersect to form a holistic understanding of Christian discipleship?

In light of these verses, how can we practically embody these principles in our relationships, attitudes, and daily choices within the church community and in our broader spheres of influence?

## Live It

This week, reach out to one of our church ministries in an active effort to promote unity. Pray for their leaders and offer them words of encouragement.

# study 8
## Philippians 2:5-8
## The Crucified God

In Paul's day emperor worship had permeated the Roman empire, requiring Roman citizens to offer incense while declaring Caesar as Lord in a Roman temple. These emperors exercised unrestrained power and dominance, particularly over the weak. Paul intentionally contrasts Jesus to these emperors by claiming that while He was equal to God and had every right to use His divine power for His own purposes, He chose humility and self-abnegation for the sake of others. He condescended to an extent that was beyond human comparison, choosing to demonstrate the true power of God through what the world would perceive as weakness. This pathway led to Christ's exaltation, providing purpose for God's people to not only praise Him but an example for them to model their lives after. This is the cruciform life. Choosing, like Jesus, humility and self-abnegation for the benefit and blessing of others.

This central theme feeds all other aspects of Paul's writing in this epistle. It is also central to every aspect of our lives. The cruciform life isn't lived from time to time or when convenient; it is a lifestyle the Christian chooses daily. This is what Jesus meant when He defined a disciple as someone who denied themselves, picked up their cross, and followed Him. It is what Paul meant when he said in Galatians 2:20 that he had been crucified with Christ. He was no longer living for Himself but living for Christ and for the sake of others.

## Pray

There is nothing theologically deeper than God becoming man and being crucified for our sakes. Understanding this is a function of revelation by God's Spirit. Spend extended time this week asking God to give you spiritual insight and understanding in this great demonstration of His humble love.

## Meditate

Direct your thoughts this week to these verses. Memorize them and repeat them over and over in your mind. As you do, expect God to draw out specific words and themes. Write them down, and at the end of the week, journal a synopsis of what God revealed to you.

## Go Deeper

Scriptures: Isaiah 53; Psalm 22:1-21; Luke 23

Connect the Old Testament Scriptures of Messiah's suffering to the New Testament story. How did the Old Testament predict Christ's suffering? How was this in conflict with what the Jews were expecting from their Messiah? How is Christ's suffering a pattern for Christian living?

## Live It

Choose to live the cruciform life this week. Be humble, deny yourself, and be willing to use your resources and opportunities as a benefit for someone else. Present yourself to God each day with this determination. When He provides the opportunity, walk in faith. At the end of each day, write down what God did through your life.

# study 9

## Philippians 2:9-11
## The Resurrected and Exalted Lord

In his magnificent hymn, Paul divides his composition into three stanzas. The first stanza speaks of the humiliation of Christ, known as kenosis, while the second elaborates on Christ's condition during His ministry. The crescendo of the hymn is the exaltation of Christ (2:9-11), marking a beautiful representation of the Christian life. Proverbs liken the path of the righteous to the increasing brightness of dawn until it becomes broad daylight.

Throughout history, figures like Abraham, Moses, David, and Jesus exemplified this pattern. Abraham left the security of his environment and was rewarded with the promised land. Moses rejected the privileges of royalty for a better citizenship. David, despite the humiliation, deepened his connection with God. Jesus, epitomizing humility, ascended to sit at the Father's right hand and was bestowed with a Name above all names.

God orchestrates a plan of exaltation for each of His children, and there is no greater high than being elevated by the Most High.

## Pray

During your prayer time, join the thousands of angels in exalting Jesus. Raise your hands, kneel, and express your deep admiration and recognition of who He is with your lips. In the end, express your devotion and surrender to Christ.

## Meditate

When Paul speaks of a "Name that is above every name," he refers to Christ's absolute authority. Take some time to meditate on what it means that Jesus has all authority over your life, the church, present events, and those to come. Consider how this truth should impact your daily life.

## Go Deeper

Scriptures: Romans 8:34; Acts 2:33; Hebrews 12:2

Considering the verses above, how should the exaltation of Christ impact your sense of present and eternal security?

What relationship do you find between the exaltation of Christ and your own exaltation? How should this impact your worship life?

## Live It

Corporate worship time is an essential part of our Sunday services. Choose to prioritize this time by participating from the beginning to the end of the service. Additionally, consider someone who needs to encounter the Jesus you worship and invite them to join you at the next Sunday service.

# study 10
## Philippians 2:12-18
## Shut Up and Shine

Paul is clear in his writings that while we don't work for our salvation, we should be working out our salvation. Simply put, all that God has worked in us through the power of Christ's gospel and the Holy Spirit should shine brightly through our lives. Paul points out this is incompatible with grumbling or disputing, which reflects a bad attitude of disappointment and a dissatisfied spirit. Paul may have in mind the children of Israel suffering through the slavery and oppression of Pharaoh, forced to make bricks with no straw and enduring the trauma of the murder of their young sons. God graciously sent them a redeemer and delivered them powerfully from Egypt, parting a sea, feeding them with Heaven's bread, and satisfying their thirst with water from a rock. Furthermore, they were miraculously led by a pillar of cloud by day and a pillar of fire by night as the Angel of the Lord made His encampment around them. Yet, for all that, they chose to grumble and dispute instead of submitting to God's chosen leader, trusting God, and giving Him thanks and praise.

Now, before you're too critical of the Israelites, consider your own life. God's deliverance has been even more remarkable for you through the Redeemer, Christ, His Son. Does your attitude reflect gratitude for all He has done? Remember, bad attitudes can dim the radiance of the light you shine for Christ. So, dial down the grumbling and complaining so you can dial up your shine for Jesus.

## Pray

Pray that God will strengthen you to experience a new season of gratitude for who He is and all He has done for you. Pray that gratitude will manifest itself in the way you see things and the words you speak.

## Meditate

Focus on Philippians 2:12-13. Meditate on this statement, "Spiritual maturity is the distance between what you know about God and how you live it out."

## Go Deeper

Scriptures: 1 Corinthians 10:9-13; Proverbs 18:21; James 3:9-10; Psalm 150:6

What emphasis does the Bible put on the words that we speak?

Do you take seriously the Scripture's warning about how we should speak?

## Live It

Shining as a light for Jesus in the darkness of our world can be as simple as honoring God with our actions and words. How will you do that this week? Write down specific actions you will take. Pray that those actions will lead to opportunities to share Jesus with people. Invite and bring someone to church this Sunday.

# key points from section 3

# section 4:
## Follow People Who Follow Jesus (2:19-30)

Influencers are people recognized for their expertise in a particular field who hold significant sway over the sometimes millions of people who flock to follow them on their platforms. Some view this as the epitome of success and dream of reaching this apex of accomplishment one day. Influencers encourage people to buy their products, vote for their politicians, believe their news, and emulate their ideas and lives. In this social media-dominated era and with accessibility to successful personalities, following examples that lead you to Jesus is more important than ever. These Jesus followers may not be known for their fashion expertise, acumen in athletics, or preeminence in politics, but if they faithfully follow Him and live His example of self-sacrifice, they are the most important influencers for you to follow.

## study 11

Philippians 2:19-30
Follow the Right Influencers

# study 11
## Philippians 2:19-30
## Follow the Right Influencers

Popular influencers often center around fashion, beauty, fitness, well-being, and travel and vacation destinations. What do these three categories share? They're all tied to temporary experiences. This highlights the prevailing priorities and values of our society.

However, followers of Jesus possess the potential to become the most impactful influencers globally. Our influence isn't rooted in popularity but in its lasting impact. As followers of Jesus, we can blaze trails in the world, and it begins by aligning ourselves with the right influencers. Paul emphasizes the importance of identifying those who are worthy of emulation and allowing them to shape our lives as Jesus has shaped them.

## Pray

Thank God for those individuals who have positively influenced your life, and ask God to empower you to be a follower of Christ who positively influences others.

## Meditate

Consider the following list: caring for others, supporting others in their calling, communicating hope, being trustworthy, prioritizing others, and selflessness. This isn't a checklist for being a Christian; instead, it outlines the characteristics of a genuine Christian influencer. Reflect on these traits and discern which resonates with you and which does not. Commit to taking steps toward embodying these qualities.

## Go Deeper

Scriptures: 1 Corinthians 15:33; Proverbs 13:20; 1 Timothy 4:12; 1 Corinthians 10:31-32

Reflecting on the preceding verses, is there any influence, whether on social media or in person, that you recognize as having a detrimental effect on your life? What action should you take to distance yourself from such influences?

We all influence those around us, but the crucial question is what type of influence we embody. Drawing from the teaching and insights found in 1 Timothy 4:12 and 1 Corinthians 10:31-32, what aspects could you integrate into your life to become a more positive and uplifting influence on those who look up to you?

## Live It

This week, take some time to send a text or a creative token of gratitude to someone who has positively influenced your life.

If your church has played a pivotal role in your spiritual journey, why not share a post about it on your social media platforms and tag the church?

# key points from section 4

# section 5:
## Seeing Your Life Through the Gospel of Christ (3:1-21)

Aviators can experience a dangerous phenomenon called spatial disorientation while flying. This occurs when the aviator loses sight of the earth and other surroundings, leading them to believe that down is up and up is down. Unfortunately, this can cause a pilot to fly their plane upside down and sometimes directly into the ground. Similarly, this upside-down flying is the natural framework through which we see our lives. Our life perspective is highly influenced by our nature, upbringing, experiences, and the worldview in which our society saturates us, clouding our understanding. We are born thinking up is down and down is up, and it isn't until we meet Jesus and have a heavenly revolution in our thinking that we see things from God's point of view as we are anchored to Christ and His truth. This transformed Paul's view of his past, present, and future. A transformation that every Christian needs as we navigate our way through this life to our eternal destiny.

**study 12**
Philippians 3:1-7
Lose It to Gain It

**study 13**
Philippians 3:8-11
A Fair Trade: My All for Christ

**study 14**
Philippians 3:12-16
Give It All You Got

**study 15**
Philippians 3:17-21
Unlock Life's Full Potential

# study 12
## Philippians 3:1-7
## Lose It to Gain It

Society says a person's value is directly connected to what they can amass for themselves. Possessions, degrees, money, experiences, followers on social media, business connections, and awards are among the many things we are encouraged to collect, with the idea that the more you have, the higher you ascend. Jesus' philosophy stood in stark contrast to this idea. Jesus told His disciples that it didn't profit a person to gain the whole world and lose their soul. He said that the one seeking to save his life would lose it, while the one who lost his life for Christ's sake and His gospel would find it. This unconventional and seemingly upside-down way of living was precisely what Paul discovered when He encountered Jesus. Paul, at that point Saul of Tarsus, had been consumed with achievements and accolades, pedigrees and persecutions. But He realized that none of his earthly accomplishments compared an iota with finding and following Jesus.

Are you caught up in the false narrative that the more you accumulate, the happier you will be or the more significant your value will be? Lose that and lean into Jesus. You will discover what is genuinely worthwhile and worth living for in Him.

## Pray

Spend extended time in prayer thanking the Father for His Son and all He's given you in Christ. Ask Him to reveal any misplaced motivations you may have in finding value and satisfaction in the world instead of in Jesus.

## Meditate

Focus on Philippians 3:7. Consider all that the Apostle Paul walked away from and how he could do that because of what He gained in Christ. How do we find value in Christ while we live in a world that preaches value from identity, achievement, and possessions?

## Go Deeper

Scriptures: Mark 8:35-37; Luke 14:33; Philippians 1:21; Matthew 4:20

Do you value what you have gained in Christ over the worldly things you possess?

How can you become more liberated from the mindset of achievement and possession as a means to value and satisfaction?

## Live It

Take bold steps like Paul did to centralize your life around Christ and all He has brought to you through His life. This may mean laying aside worldly pursuits that have consumed your attention and instead leaning into Jesus and living for Him and His gospel.

# study 13

## Philippians 3:8-11
## A Fair Trade: My All for Christ

The themes Paul addresses in this brief passage are deeply profound, resonating with the aspirations of believers since the dawn of Christianity. To truly know Jesus, to treasure Him above all else, to embody God's justice, to partake in the transformative power of Christ's resurrection, and ultimately, to mirror His victory over death—these are the pursuits that define our faith journey. Such lofty aspirations are within reach; all it takes is a small yet significant exchange—surrendering our all to gain Him fully. Are you willing to make this exchange?

For Paul, the exchange was a no-brainer and a bargain. Yet, for many, the idea of sacrificing all for Christ is daunting and seemingly too high a price. What sets Paul apart is his acceptance that his identity is enfolded in Christ; everything else pales in comparison to the transformative journey of becoming like Jesus.

## Pray

Pray for God's revelation of the surpassing value of your identity in Christ that He would unveil the true nature of earthly pursuits, revealing their insignificance compared to the richness of Christ and His blessings.

## Meditate

Paul employs the term " huperechó" to convey the outcome of his experience—a comparison between the qualities of two entities to discern which one surpasses the other. The aspects that filled Paul with pride prior to following Jesus weren't inherently negative. For instance, belonging to an influential ethnic group with sway in both religious and political spheres could be considered a commendable pursuit. However, the conclusion became unmistakable upon consciously evaluating his past in light of Christ.

Take a moment to reflect and assess your values juxtaposed to Christ's. Do you arrive at a realization similar to Paul's?

## Go Deeper

Scriptures: Romans 12:1; Galatians 2:20; Matthew 6:19-21; 2 Corinthians 9:7

Based on these verses, we find not a formula but rather a constant: comparison, surrender, and experience. What aspects of your life need testing against the eternal? What needs surrendering? Which aspects of the Christian life are you yet to experience?

## Live It

Ensuring our values are aligned with God's is vital. For assistance, consider evaluating your values at *lifevaluesinventory.org*.

After your assessment, discuss your results with a friend or a leader and develop an action plan to align your values with Christ's.

# study 14
## Philippians 3:12-16
## Give It All You Got

If you have played sports, you know it takes your total effort throughout the game to get away with the win. I recently heard a well-known NBA player acknowledge this by affirming that winning the game takes total effort over 48 minutes. That takes determination, commitment, and stamina. It means that you can't be half-hearted or lazy. You have to give it all you got to come away with the win.

Paul understood this to be the case with the Christian life. As accomplished as Paul was in his spiritual maturity and ministry exploits, he knew he hadn't arrived. The goal was still set before him, and Paul pursued it with everything he had. Instead of resting on his laurels, the grand accomplishments of his past, he chose not to consider them so that he could strain forward, like a runner stretching his whole body out to gain one more inch to bring him the win.

That was the effort that Paul put into his Christian life. How about you?

## Pray

Begin your time in prayer, thanking God for all He has done in and through your life. Confess your desire to press on even harder, asking for the strength and the will to run your race with endurance.

## Meditate

Focus on Philippians 3:13-14. Based on these verses, how did Paul view his past, present, and future? Paul committed severe sins against God and his church as a persecutor. Do you think Paul lived in freedom from his past? If so, how?

## Go Deeper

Scriptures: Hebrews 11:1-12:1; Luke 9:59-62

It is easy to rest in your past spiritual and kingdom accomplishments and begin to coast instead of straining forward. What does that difference practically look like?

What did Paul have in mind when he spoke of the prize of the upward call of God in Christ Jesus as our goal?

## Live It

Be intentionally encouraging to at least three Christians this week, to run their race wholeheartedly, who seem to be coasting. Pray together and ask God to reignite the fire in your hearts.

# study 15
## Philippians 3:17-21
## Unlock Life's Full Potential

When I was young, I was a fan of video games. It was always thrilling to reach a level where the game allowed me to "unlock a new character." This signaled an improvement in my gameplay and promised an exciting new adventure to conquer. Despite Paul's current condition when writing Philippians (imprisonment), his words are imbued with depth and purpose, as if he has "unlocked a new character" in his walk with Jesus.

In today's text, Paul warns against those who opt for the easy path of self-indulgence and pleasure, leading to an ordinary, purposeless, and sterile existence. Simultaneously, he invites his readers to "unlock" a new lifestyle characterized by purpose and power in the present, with hope for the future. By unlocking God's full potential for your life, you can embark on a new stage characterized by power, joy, and fruitfulness in order to experience real spiritual growth in Jesus.

## Pray

Pray for God to ignite within you a spiritual ambition, an unquenchable thirst to know Him, and faithfully walk alongside Christ intimately. Seek His guidance to discern the areas where impulses rather than His Spirit have led you. Finally, ask God to help you infuse Heaven's perspective into every dimension of your existence.

## Meditate

Reflect on the following: on one hand, some disdain the cross of Christ, whom Paul describes as worshipping their own desires. On the other hand, individuals like Samuel Rutherford, echoing Paul's sentiments, express a profound appreciation for the cross. Rutherford wrote, "The cross of Christ is the sweetest burden that I ever bore; it is such a burden as wings are to a bird, or sails to a ship, to carry me forward to my harbor." What distinguishes these two perspectives? With which do you resonate?

## Go Deeper

Scriptures: Philippians 3:20; John 10:10; Jeremiah 29:11; Proverbs 3:5-6

Based on these verses, how can you create and keep an eternal mindset?

Drawing from these verses, extract four keys that will help you unlock life's full potential.

## Live It

Conduct a distraction inventory: Compile a list of 10 things that might be diverting your focus from God's potential for your life. Then, in prayer, seek God's wisdom to discern and address these distractions effectively.

# key points from section 5

# section 6:
## Right Side Up Your Thinking (4:1-9)

The Proverbs reminds us that as a man thinks, so he is. In other words, how we think radically influences the quality and even the course of our lives. Now, when the gospel turns the framework through which we see our lives right side up, it transforms how we think. Our mindset takes a heavenly turn towards what pleases God and what brings genuine flourishing to our lives. Paul discovered this truth and lived it out in the challenging circumstance of imprisonment because of his faith in Jesus. Even in this tribulation, Paul flourished because he chose to rejoice in adversity, pray in painful circumstances, and focus his thoughts on those things that pleased God. The mind truly is a battleground, but when we fight with the weapons God gives us, we experience the flourishing life through God's grace and the power of His Spirit.

### study 16
Philippians 4:1-7
The Great Exchange

### study 17
Philippians 4:8-9
Psychological Warfare

# study 16
## Philippians 4:1-7
## The Great Exchange

Anxiety seems to be taking our society by almost epidemic proportions. In a recent survey, nearly 4 in 10 adults reported symptoms of anxiety or depression. Moreover, according to a recent article in Forbes, 19.1 million Americans are struggling with various anxiety disorders.[2] While Americans wrestle with solutions to their anxiety, the Scripture gives us the first and most important step we can take, and that is prayer. In one of the most profound and powerful verses written by the Apostle Paul, prayer is presented as the antidote to anxiety. Communion with the Father and unburdening the various stressors in your life into His Almighty care produces the profound peace of God that sets itself like a sentinel around your heart.

This week, resist the temptation to bury your anxiety in a Netflix binge or a shopping spree. Instead, pour yourself into a meaningful time of prayer and supplication and experience the great exchange of your anxiety for His peace.

## Pray

Take steps this week to dedicate considerable time to prayer. Intentionally, remove distractions and use that time to draw closer to God. Write down the list of things stressing you out and entrust them to Him with gratitude.

## Meditate

Focus on Philippians 4:6-7. Memorize these verses. How does trusting God with the struggles in your life lead to peace? Why does Paul add the word, thanksgiving, to qualify prayers and supplications? Why is giving thanks to God important, and how is it connected to God's peace?

## Go Deeper

Scriptures: 1 Peter 5:6-7; John 14:27; Matthew 6:25-34; Proverbs 12:25

According to the Bible, what negative impact does anxiety have on our lives?

What are the true Christian responses to anxiety and stress?

## Live It

Reach out to people in your life struggling with anxiety. Ask them how you can pray for them. Be merciful to them in their struggle.

# study 17
## Philippians 4:8-9
## Psychological Warfare

In prison, Paul faced not only the internal struggles of his mind but also relentless psychological attacks from external sources. These assaults came in various forms: the pessimism of some fellow believers, the ridicule of his opponents, the threats from the Roman guards, and the distressing reports from the churches he had founded. It amounted to a veritable "Psychological Warfare."

Similarly, Christians in the 21st century find themselves in comparable circumstances. We are confronted with sophisticated propaganda aimed at manipulating our perceptions, faith, and behavior. However, Paul offers us a powerful weapon that can alter the course of this battle: "We, as children of God, possess the power of the Holy Spirit to choose our thoughts." This message is both empowering and brimming with hope.

## Pray

Express gratitude to God for His Holy Spirit while simultaneously seeking His empowerment to overcome the psychological warfare you encounter.

## Meditate

Observe the text and note that Paul uses the word "whatever" six times, suggesting many possibilities. It's intriguing that amidst overwhelming thoughts, we often overlook the array of positive alternatives God has provided for every negative occurrence. Allow the peace of God to permeate your being as you reflect on the abundance of blessings and virtues awaiting you in Christ.

## Go Deeper

Scriptures: Colossians 3:2; 2 Corinthians 10:5; Ephesians 6:17; Isaiah 26:3

What do these verses teach you about overcoming the battle of your mind?

On a scale from 1 to 3, where 1 represents not at all responsible, 2 signifies some responsibility, and 3 denotes complete responsibility, consider your accountability for your thoughts. According to scripture, what steps can you take to enhance your responsibility for your thoughts?

## Live It

This week, implement these three steps to experience victory in the battle for your mind:

- Reject all narratives (internal or external) that promote division and fear.
- Rewind your mind: Assess and discard divisive, destructive, and spiritually alien thoughts and influences through the guidance of the Holy Spirit.
- Renew your mind: Immerse yourself in truth—His Word, praise, and gratitude—to rejuvenate your thoughts.

# key points from section 6

# section 7:
## Living a Content Life in Christ (4:10-23)

On September 1, 1985, the Titanic, the infamous unsinkable ship that ran into an iceberg and sank 13,000 feet in the freezing waters of the North Atlantic, was at last discovered. It's not that the ship hadn't been there, rusting away year after year; it's just that finding it proved exceedingly difficult. Countless efforts had been made but to no avail, as this hulking mass of steel illusively evaded the many attempts. Contentment can prove as challenging to find as the Titanic. No matter how hard you look for it, it never seems to be where you think it should be. In the ocean of options, only one thing stands approved by God and time-tested as the true source of satisfaction: Jesus Christ. He has always been there waiting for you to discover and experience Him. Contentment is yours to experience; all you must do is look in the right place.

### study 18
Philippians 4:10-13
Content!

### study 19
Philippians 4:14-20
Gospel Giving Partnerships

### study 20
Philippians 4:21-23
Trophies of Grace

# study 18
## Philippians 4:10-13
## Content!

If I had a dollar for every time I saw Philippians 4:13 tattooed on someone, I wouldn't be rich, but let's say I would have enough money to buy my coffee for the rest of the year. It is an excellent verse without question and is used for all sorts of contexts. Athletes use it to describe the physical strength God gives them to compete. Students use it when depending on God to help them ace their tests. Pastors use it when taking an audacious step of faith to advance the ministry. And while Christ does give us strength to do all those things, this verse refers to something different altogether. It refers to the strength Christ gives us to be content in Him regardless of our circumstances. From house arrest in Rome, Paul uttered words that have eluded the greatest minds of our age: the key to true contentment.

Contentment isn't found in your possessions, retirement, an aesthetic lifestyle, or from within. It is found in Jesus. It is by His enabling strength that you can live with this extraordinary freedom.

## Pray

Be intentional this week to close each day out in prayer. Consider the day's events and thank God for His faithful involvement in your life. Count the blessings He has given you, and confess your contentment in Him.

## Meditate

Focus on Philippians 4:11. Think more deeply about what Paul means when he says he learned to be content. How did Paul learn to be content? Using the Blue Letter Bible, do a word study on the word *rejoice*.

## Go Deeper

Scriptures: Matthew 11:28-30; 1 Timothy 6:6-10; John 6:68

How do we find true satisfaction in Christ?

What steps can you take to depend on Christ's power to strengthen you completely?

## Live It

Share an encouraging story of how Jesus gave you strength when you desperately needed it. (*share at awakenlv.org/kenosis*)

# study 19
## Philippians 4:14-20
## Gospel Giving Partnerships

The Philippian church distinguished itself among the other churches Paul planted by recognizing its role as a partner in advancing the kingdom. Within this small congregation, we discover a model we can call "Gospel Giving Partnerships": One receives the vision, the church rallies behind it with prayer and financial support, others join in the evangelistic endeavor, God receives glory, the church experiences blessings, and the gospel is proclaimed.

So, what enables a church to fulfill its intended purpose? I would assert that it's the dedication of its members. A church requires a Pastor like Paul, unwavering in preaching the gospel; individuals like Epaphroditus, steadfast in supporting the church's efforts and vision; and members like the Philippians, steadfast in their commitment to uphold the vision and work to which God has called them.

## Pray

In your prayer, express gratitude to God for all He accomplished through Awaken last year. Ask Him to reveal the role He wants you to play in extending His kingdom in Las Vegas and beyond in the coming year.

## Meditate

Reflect on verse 18 and consider how Paul describes the Philippians' generosity as "a fragrant offering, a sacrifice acceptable and pleasing to God." Then, contemplate the connection between these offerings, the blessings mentioned in verse 19, and the glory that God receives through them.

## Go Deeper

Scriptures: 1 Corinthians 3:9-10; 2 Corinthians 9:7; 2 Corinthians 8:12; Proverbs 11:24

How are you putting gospel collaboration at the center of your relationships with believers? How are you putting gospel priorities at the center of your financial and prayer life?

## Live It

Reflect on Sunday's message and your personal study. Ask God to reveal how you can actively support the church's vision and mission in practical ways, such as serving in a ministry, going on a mission trip, or volunteering at LV Reach. If you haven't already, consider beginning to partner with God and the church financially (10% is a good start).

# study 20
## Philippians 4:21-23
## Trophies of Grace

I played a lot of soccer growing up, which was about 19 years' worth. As a result, I had countless trophies in my room. Not because I was "so good" but because I always seemed to play on good teams. Each trophy had a special meaning. Maybe it was an incredibly challenging year, but we pressed through and made it to the finals. Or a tournament we traveled to, where we even surprised ourselves and took first place. The point is that each trophy had a unique story, which is true with every child of God. Each of us is a trophy of God's grace. We have our own story of how God graciously rescued us and how He demonstrates His faithfulness to us daily. Every story is unique because each of us matters to God. We are valuable in His sight and have inestimable worth. Furthermore, each story is unique because our story is really about God and all He did for us through Jesus, His Son.

Paul was writing to a church in Philippi, a city inhabited by retired Roman soldiers familiar with the victory procession of conquering generals through the streets of Rome. Riding a four-horse chariot, these generals would lead the procession as their soldiers followed along with the captives and the spoils of war. Christ is our victor. He has conquered sin, death, and hell and made us trophies of His grace. One day, we will march with Him in that heavenly procession as citizens of the celestial city, clothed in white garments and singing His praise throughout eternity.

## Pray

Allocate a few hours this week to write down your personal story of how God intervened in your life, revealed Himself, and rescued you. Be specific about the details before you believed in Jesus, and also be specific about all He has done after you received Jesus.

## Meditate

Focus on Philippians 4:21-22. Every saint mattered to Paul, and every saint matters to God. Reflect on the value and worth you have in God's eyes. Do you carry that value over to other Christians and see them as valuable in God's eyes?

## Go Deeper

Scriptures: Ephesians 1:4; Ephesians 2:10; Revelation 1:6; Titus 2:11-14

How does Christ's atonement establish our value/worth?

## Live It

Share the personal testimony you wrote down during your prayer time this week with someone at work, on social media, or in another way. Be prepared to lead someone in prayer to receive Christ, just as you have.

# key points from section 7

# Conclusion

We are grateful to have been able to dig deep with you into the book of Philippians. Thank you for joining us on this journey. A journey that has enabled us to fulfill the mission of Awaken, which is to be a community of Jesus followers who worship God, grow as disciples, and reach Las Vegas and the world with the gospel of Jesus Christ. Carry forward what God has taught you as you seek to faithfully reach people with Christ's love so they can become a part of God's family.

# about the authors

Derek Neider & Fernando Serrano

Derek Neider is the Lead Pastor of Awaken Las Vegas, a multi-congregational Christian church in Las Vegas, Nevada, and part of the Awaken Church Community. He is also the President of Awaken Events, which are large-scale evangelistic events and humanitarian outreaches that unite local churches, reach the lost, and equip God's people. He is passionate about helping people grow in their relationship with Jesus, church planting, and fulfilling the Great Commission worldwide.

Derek and his wife, Rachel, have three amazing children: Alec and his wife Arianna, Hanna, and Levi.

Fernando Serrano is the founder of Awaken Oasis, a vibrant bilingual church in North Las Vegas. Originally from Mexico, Fernando and his family moved to Las Vegas to foster spiritual growth within the city's diverse community. Awaken Oasis is part of the Awaken Church Community. Passionate about spreading the Gospel of Jesus Christ, Fernando is committed to making an impact both locally and globally.

Fernando lives in Las Vegas with his wife Liliana and cherishes his role as a father to Keren, Dan, Josías, and Valeria, as well as a father-in-law to Noe and Natalie. Their joy is completed by their granddaughter, Aria.

f ⊙ @derekneider

f ⊙ @pastorfernny

# Endnotes

1          (Pogosyan, Marianna. "The Power of Believing in Yourself" Psychology Today, July 22, 2022 https://www.psychologytoday.com/us/blog/between-cultures/202207/the-power-believing-in-yourself) defined confidence as a belief in oneself, the conviction that one has the ability to meet life's challenges and succeed—and the willingness to act accordingly. Another article on the same website said, "self-confidence is linked to almost every element involved in a happy and fulfilling life." (Markway, Barbara. "Why Self-Confidence Is More Important Than You Think", Psychologoy Today, September 20, 2018. https://www.psychologytoday.com/us/blog/shyness-is-nice/201809/why-self-confidence-is-more-important-you-think )

2          (Booth, Jessica. Anxiety Statistics And Facts, "Forbes Health" October 23, 2023 https://www.forbes.com/health/mind/anxiety-statistics/)

Made in the USA
Columbia, SC
08 August 2024